P9-DNQ-615

THE SOFT LIZARDS

What do you think of when you hear the word gecko? If you are like most people with even a passing interest in keeping lizards, you probably envision one of the four most common groups of these lizards: leopards, fat-tails, tokays, or day geckos. However, readily available and quite keepable groups. All the geckos are interesting to the specialist, even if they are only 3 inches long and plain as dirt, but space of course forces us to limit our discussions to about a dozen groups or genera.

This Moorish Gecko, *Tarentola mauritanica*, exhibits many of the characteristics typical of the geckos: vertical pupils, tubercular scales, enlarged toe-pads, and a large head and mouth. Photo by J. Merli.

the geckos are very diverse lizards that can be divided into two distinctive families and at least 700 species, so obviously there are many other lesser known geckos to whet the interest of the beginning or advanced lizard keeper. In this book we hope to introduce you to the group and its general care as pets, not only reacquainting you with the four major types you probably already know, but mentioning a few other

WHAT IS A GECKO?

First, let's get the formalities out of the way. Just what kind of lizard are we talking about when we talk about geckos? If you think of geckos as soft lizards, you won't be that far wrong. Though the geckos are scientifically defined by differences of the bones of the skull and body skeleton, among other characters, hobbyists can only look at a lizard from the outside. While most lizards are covered with rather large and prominent scales that overlap at the edges like fish scales and often have bony cores, geckos usually have tiny scales that look more like raised pimples and goosebumps than the scales of a fish. Often the skin itself is very soft, delicate, loose, and easily torn, the scattered enlarged tubercles doing little to strengthen it. While most lizards depend on the thickness of their scales for protection from predators, geckos depend on their subtle camouflage colors (cryptic coloration) and secretive nature to avoid predators.

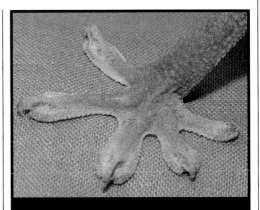

Notice the enlarged toe-pads on the foot of this White-striped Gecko, *Gekko vittatus*. These adaptations allow geckos to run up and down very smooth surfaces—sometimes across ceilings! Photo by W. P. Mara.

As a rule, the undersides of the fingers and toes of geckos have at least a few pads of microscopic hair-like projections (cilia) that allow them to grasp the most minute of cracks and irregularities as they climb. These climbing pads give geckos (and, of course, several other types of lizards, such as the anoles) an

Close-up of a Tokay Gecko, *Gekko gecko*. The fine scales interspersed with tubercular ones are plainly visible. Also obvious is the attractive coloration of this popular gecko. Photo by W.P. Mara.

Most geckos are nocturnal and have vertical pupils. The iris is often beautifully colored with intricate marbling. This is a New Caledonian gecko, *Rhacodactylus chahoua.* Photo by M. Bacon.

advantage over many other lizards, letting them climb smooth vertical surfaces as they chase prey or escape from predators, or even chase each other around during mating. Though they often are called adhesive pads, there is little evidence to show that any type of glue is secreted by the pads. Not all geckos have pads, of course, and the terrestrial (ground-living) types often lack the pads entirely or are in the process of losing them.

Geckos have large eyes with large pupils. The majority of geckos are active at night (nocturnal) or at dawn and dusk (crepuscular) and, as is usual in animals active during the dark, they have vertical pupils. Unlike the normal cat-eye pupils of most other nocturnal lizards, however, the pupils of geckos often are elaborated with scallops and semicircles. When the gecko is exposed to bright light and the pupil contracts into a narrow vertical slit, the scallops from opposite sides meet and leave tiny pinholes in the closed pupil that apparently allow geckos to see even with their eyes closed. In most geckos there are three or four sets of pinholes, producing a very distinctive appearance that is typical of gecko eyes. The iris of the gecko eye often is brightly patterned with gold and silver reticulations and fine lines. Many hobbyists feel that the eyes of a gecko are its finest feature, and even dull brown geckos may have beautiful golden, orange, silver, or even green eyes.

Geckos have large, rather fleshy tongues that have a short slit at the tip. The tongue is flexible, allowing the lizards to quickly flick up small insects or drops of nectar and fruit juices. Most geckos can be seen to lick their eyes on occasion, probably to simply help clean them of small particles of dirt and sand. Geckos have relatively large, quite functional teeth and the heavy jaw muscles to make them useful. All geckos can produce a good pinch when they bite your finger, and some of the large species (especially the tokays, genus *Gekko*) not only grab on, but also twist the head, tearing the skin and drawing blood.

Finally, geckos are notorious for their ability to drop their tail. The process of voluntarily breaking off the tail is known as autotomy and is found in many lizards. Most geckos have rather thick, fleshy tails that in species from dry habitats may contain special cells that allow storage of water and fatty fluids during periods of abundance so they can be used during emergencies. The original tail of many geckos is covered with distinctive scales that may be in circular patterns (whorls) and quite different in appearance from the scales of the body. When a predator attacks—such as your gently grasping hand during cage cleaning—the gecko tenses sets of muscles just beyond the base of the tail that lie over a specially thinned bony area of one of the

While most geckos can regenerate lost tails, the replacement is rarely as long and colorful as the original. This Seipp's Day Gecko, *Phelsuma seippi*, has a new tail that fails to blend in with its otherwise attractive colors. Photo by I. Francais.

The Desert Banded Gecko, *Coleonyx variegatus*, is an example of the eyelid geckos. Many scientists place the eyelid geckos in a separate family, Eublepharidae. Photo by Z. Takacs.

tail vertebrae. This area is known as the fracture plane or seam of the vertebra, and the bone actually separates at this point, allowing the tail to drop off and continue thrashing about as the gecko runs off. Special constrictures in the blood vessels prevent excessive bleeding. Some geckos, such as the Turkish Gecko, *Hemidactylus turcicus*, are especially bad about dropping their tails. A small colony we keep always seems to have more animals lacking tails than those with them. Fortunately, a well-fed gecko quickly regenerates a new tail (in *Hemidactylus* and *Coleonyx* the tail grows so fast you can actually see the growth from day to day, with a full tail forming in just a few weeks), though it usually is stouter than the original, may have a different color pattern than normal, and lacks any specialized scales present in the original. In nature, repeated loss of the tail may endanger the life of a gecko, as it deprives the animal of stored water and fat and forces the lizard to burn calories to regenerate the tail.

GECKO CLASSIFICATIONS

The general definition of a gecko given above of course cannot hope to encompass all the variations present in this group. Over 700, and probably closer to 800, species are described (with more new ones discovered each year), but exactly how they are related to each other remains conjectural and a source of argument among herpetologists (scientists who study reptiles and amphibians). Traditionally, all the geckos have been placed in a single family, the Gekkonidae, considered to be closely related to both the Australian snake-lizards, the Pygopodidae, and the American night lizards, Xantusiidae. The Gekkonidae was broken into two major groups called subfamilies, one with movable eyelids (the Eublepharinae, including the leopard geckos and allies) and one without eyelids (the Gekkoninae, including the tokays and other typical geckos). The eyelid geckos differ in so many aspects of their skeleton and show such a great similarity to each other in general form and even color patterns that today the following genera, all with movable eyelids, are considered to form the full family Eublepharidae:

- *Aeluroscalabotes*, the cat geckos of Thailand, Malaysia, and Borneo
- *Coleonyx*, the banded geckos of the southwestern United States, Mexico, and Central America
- *Goniurosaurus*, the Oriental

The hardy and beautiful Leopard Gecko, *Eublepharis macularius*, is the most popular of all geckos. Virtually all the Leopard Geckos available are captive bred. Photo by I. Francais.

Diplodactylus ciliaris, the Spiny-tailed Gecko, is often placed in a subfamily that includes the New Zealand geckos and, according to some researchers, the serpentine pygopodid lizards. Photo by Z. Takacs.

leopard geckos from the Ryukyus, Hainan, and other islands

- *Eublepharis*, the leopard geckos found from India to Iraq and Iran
- *Hemitheconyx*, the fat-tailed geckos from eastern and western Africa
- *Holodactylus*, the whole-toed geckos of dry northeastern Africa.

All the other geckos, some 80 to 90 genera and over 700 species, are placed in the family Gekkonidae, all the species of which lack movable eyelids and instead have the eye covered with a single transparent scale known as a brille or spectacle. Several smaller groups are recognized in

Bibron's Gecko, *Pachydactylus bibroni*, is a fairly typical gecko with large eyes and well-developed climbing abilities. They are quite hardy. Photo by I. Francais.

the Gekkonidae, but they are of little concern to the average hobbyist. The small ground and reef geckos of tropical America are placed in a subfamily Sphaerodactylinae, while a group of odd Australian geckos in which glands in the tail of some species can spew out a noxious white chemical is placed as the subfamily Diplodactylinae (this subfamily includes the giant geckos, *Rhacodactylus*, and the rare imports from New Guinea of *Lialis burtonis*, a pretty species that feeds mostly on other lizards. What makes these lizards important to gecko enthusiasts is that recently some herpetologists have considered them to be geckos rather than a separate family. When all the data from the skeleton and soft tissues are analyzed in a certain way, it appears that the subfamily Diplodactylinae of the geckos is

The pygopodid lizards have traditionally been given their own family, Pygopodidae. New research suggests they may be a subfamily of the geckos. This is the Hooded Scaly-foot, *Pygopus nigriceps*. Photo by K. W. Switak.

New Zealand geckos as well).

In Australia and New Guinea there are several types of snake-like lizards that have the front legs absent and the hind legs reduced to tiny flaps near the vent. These are the pygopodids or snake-lizards. Hobbyists see few of these lizards other than a few more closely related to the pygopodids than to the rest of the geckos. Some workers would then take the diplodactylins and place them with the pygopodids as a separate family containing ordinary looking geckos and snake-like forms. Other workers view the same evidence as a

To many people the Tokay Gecko, *Gekko gecko*, is the quintessential gecko. Keeping in mind its large size, bold colors, draconian eyes, and aggressive personality, it's easy to see this viewpoint. Photo by I. Francais.

reason to bring the snake-lizards into the family Gekkonidae. Neither new grouping seems especially convincing, and in this book we'll stick to the old classification and recognize separate families for the "normal" geckos that have four legs and the snake-lizards with their greatly reduced, almost invisible legs.

IDENTIFYING GECKOS

At the moment, there is no book that discusses and illustrates all the species of geckos. Considering how popular these lizards have become in the last decade, this problem should be remedied soon. However, at the moment identification of most geckos is difficult or impossible, especially if you have just one or two living specimens, probably immature, purchased as unknown species from an uncertain locality. Many of the characters of a gecko are in its feet, so it doesn't hurt to look carefully as the feet first. Does the gecko have pads under all the toes or just some? Are the pads divided in the center, single, or split into three? Is there a claw at the tip of the digit, and is it covered with special scales? Many of these characters can be seen as a gecko adheres to the glass of its terrarium, and some can even be made out in the shed skin. Notice also just how the scales on the back are arranged: are they regular, are large tubercles scattered over the back, or are the tubercles in regular rows? Do the scales on the tail (if not regenerated) form regular rows?

The scales at the edges of the lips often are distinctive in certain groups of geckos, as are the scales around the nostrils. Do the eyes have special scales around them, such as fringes to help keep out sand? How is the pupil shaped? Is it round (uncommon in geckos) or a vertical slit, and if a slit, how many pinholes are there?

Color patterns in geckos often are misleading, as unrelated geckos often share similar patterns. Many have a pale curved line behind the head (the nuchal loop) and broad dark bands across the back. Additionally, in perhaps most geckos the pattern changes with growth, young specimens often being banded and adults being spotted, striped, plain, or variously banded. Try to keep a photographic record of your unknown gecko as it grows both in order to help you identify it later and to perhaps add information to the body of knowledge about uncommon geckos.

If you want to learn more about geckos, there is no shortage of books on the subject. Try Seufer's *Keeping and Breeding Geckos* (T.F.H. Publ.) for a well-illustrated introduction. Magazine articles on geckos are common, and they often appear in *Reptile Hobbyist*. There even is a society devoted strictly to the study of geckos, the International Gecko Society, that publishes a small journal known as *Dactylus*. There probably are between 500 and 1000 hobbyists

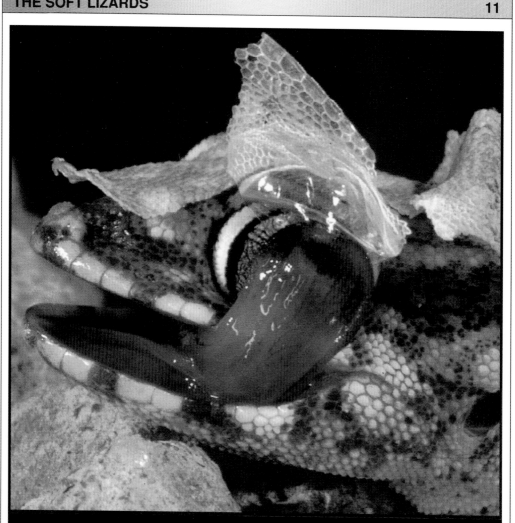

Many geckos use their tongue to clean dirt from the brille covering their eyes. This is the Israeli Desert Gecko, *Stenodactylus petri*. Photo by Z. Takacs.

specializing in breeding and studying geckos, and they enable importers and commercial breeders to provide a great number of different geckos to the pet shop and specialist dealers in reptiles. A few visits to your pet shop are sure to let you see half a dozen different species in a short while, and a visit to a local or regional reptile show will set your mouth watering for the rare, expensive, and truly strange geckos you will see there.

So start off easy, with a Leopard or Fat-tail, and let your accumulating experience lead you into ever more strange and uncommon species. Though most hobbyists want to breed their geckos, this should not be considered necessary, though it is good experience. Enjoy your charges for what they are— strange, occasionally colorful, sometimes delicate, and usually friendly little visitors to your terraria.

THE FAMILY PET

First, we prefer to think of our geckos as pets, not specimens. Though they have no choice as to the directions of their lives, they really are our guests; though we own them, they are more our responsibilities than just objects to be possessed. It has been said that much can be determined about a person by the way their pets are treated. Though they are not cuddly and hairy like cats and dogs, your geckos are your pets and deserve your full respect.

Obviously it is somewhat misleading to generalize about the methods of care, feeding, and breeding of a group with over 700 species found over most of the tropical and subtropical areas of the world. The following sections present some general rules for gecko care; for details you must see the chapters on the specific animals. Desert geckos will need different substrates and watering cycles than will rainforest species, of course, but it shouldn't take a

This hatchling Desert Banded Gecko, *Coleonyx variegatus*, will need to be fed very tiny insects. Many hatchling geckos are smaller than full-grown crickets! Photo by R. D. Bartlett.

Sand is a good substrate for desert-dwelling geckos, like this Leopard Gecko, *Eublepharis macularius*. Playground sand is safe, and, recently, sands specifically for reptiles have become available at pet stores. Photo by I. Francais.

genius to determine where general rules won't apply. If at all possible, keep your setup simple, clean it regularly, and observe the behavior of your geckos. Don't worry too much about illnesses, because there is little you can do about a disease if it strikes, and a gecko that is well-cared-for stays healthy. If you notice mites, see your pet shop for an effective remedy. If you have wild-caught geckos, see your veterinarian about worming.

THE TERRARIUM

Gecko keepers are lucky because their pets fit well into the cheap, easily purchased all-glass aquaria sold in any pet shop. Unless you are keeping a very large species or one that likes to climb about in rainforest trees, this will do fine. A 10-gallon tank is roomy enough for a trio (a male and two females) of adult Leopard Geckos, and a 20-gallon tank can house a similar group of Tokay Geckos. The aquarium must have a sturdy lid that is at least half screened to allow proper ventilation and also serve as a platform for the light.

Also satisfactory for non-climbing geckos such as Leopards and Fat-tails are plastic shoe boxes and sweater boxes. Many pet shops now stock these boxes. They come with lids that should have the center cut out and replaced with a rectangle of very fine-mesh fiberglass screen (use duct tape to attach the screen). Geckos from dry areas cannot tolerate humidity, which will rapidly build up in a shoe box with just a few holes punched along the sides and lid. If you are keeping geckos from more moist habitats, a piece of glass or plastic can be placed over part of the screen to help control moisture levels in the box. These boxes are of course not as visually desirable as tanks and are too shallow for many geckos, but they are cheap and stackable, as well as being very light in

Here is an elaborate and attractive setup suitable for forest-dwelling geckos. Live plants provide climbing surfaces and help retain humidity. The digital thermometer facilitates a close monitoring of the temperature. Photo by J. LePage.

weight, which makes cleaning easier.

If you are keeping large numbers of Leopard Geckos or a similar species, you might want to invest in a rack system that allows you to keep many shoe boxes on shallow shelves along a wall. Some systems are designed to hold boxes without lids, relying on the close fit of the box against the shelf above it to keep in any escape artists. Dozens of trios and their young can be kept in a very small area. Some pet shops now handle such racks, and many will be glad to check into ordering one for you. Manufacturers also advertise in the reptile magazines. Again, if you just have a few geckos that you want to display, racks are not for you.

Many hobbyists like the appearance of specially built vertical terraria of plexiglass, plastic, and rich wood edging. These terraria may be quite expensive to purchase, but they usually are well-built and will last many years. They can be customized for various types of lighting and heating setups and even for automatic misting units for rainforest geckos. They are indeed a wonderful luxury, but they are not essential for you to enjoy your pet—think of them as the equivalent of a heated, air conditioned doghouse.

BEDDING

Hobbyists have argued for decades over the best substrates or bedding materials for reptile cages. Some love sand, others say sand causes gut impactions. Wood chips are fine for some keepers, but others say they are just excellent hiding places for mites. (All keepers agree that cedar should never be used because the volatile oils given off by cedar chips are believed to cause tumors and other problems in cold-blooded pets.) Some hobbyists have had excellent luck with newspaper, paper towels, or squares of all-weather carpeting (not the green plastic artificial grass carpets that are sharp and may cause abrasions on the feet and bellies of delicate lizards), while others consider them totally unnatural and to be avoided at all cost.

The secret of bedding is to use what works for you, not for someone else. Experience shows that Leopard and Banded Geckos do very well on a substrate of fine playbox sand only an inch or so deep—they are not burrowers in the terrarium and seem to have no problem grabbing dry crickets without eating too much sand. Fat-tails like it a bit more moist and do well on a mixture of sand and vermiculite or just vermiculite that is kept just barely moist by regular sprayings. Small geckos from moist habitats do best on a substrate of potting soil mixed with peat or sphagnum.

The proper bedding must retain the correct amount of moisture for the lizard without becoming too wet. It should provide a stable base for decorations and hiding places. Lastly, it must be easy to clean and not promote the rapid growth of fungus and bacteria on feces. (It also helps if it doesn't provide crickets with too many hiding places.) Match the substrate to the gecko.

Packaged beddings are convenient and inexpensive. Most are attractive and can be cleaned and reused. They are available at many pet stores. Photo: courtesy of Tetra/Second Nature.

DECORATIONS

All terraria look better with an interesting background, such as the printed scenes sold in many pet shops; these colorful sheets can be found to match the tastes of any keeper. (Don't worry, the geckos cannot visualize a printed surface and thus are not annoyed by any color pattern you might choose.) Background sheets keep light from entering the terrarium from the back and sides and thus give the geckos more security. If you wish to make up your own background from painted Styrofoam, cork sheeting, or plastic plates, just remember that if you put it inside the terrarium you are asking for trouble in the form of feces deposits, hidden dead crickets, and perhaps uncontrollable hiding places for climbing geckos that will allow them to stay out of sight all the time. Keep it simple!

All geckos want hiding places for when they are not active or for when they believe they are challenged by a predator (you, of course). We are partial to curved

This small terrarium for Leopard Geckos, *Eublepharis macularius*, includes a humidified shelter. Lightly misting it with water a few times a week will keep it moist enough. Photo by I. Francais.

pieces of cork bark, a natural substance that is cheap to purchase, easily broken into various sizes and shapes, and survives repeated soakings in bleach to keep it clean. Ceramic hide boxes can be purchased in various sizes and also are easy to keep clean. Avoid cheap hide boxes that cannot survive bleach. Small geckos often will use the little black plastic canisters that house 35mm camera film.

Climbing geckos need branches on which to climb. Be sure the branches are securely anchored so they cannot fall and crush a lizard, and also be sure that the upper end of the branch does not come too close to the terrarium edge to aid escapers in their endeavors. You can cut your own branches (dead branches are better than live ones because all the sap has been leached from them) or buy them from a pet shop. Be sure to soak all branches for at least an hour in a bleach solution to kill any mites or their eggs that might be present—mites love to live under small bark fragments.

Living plants look good but are a pain to keep in the average terrarium. Geckos (except day geckos, *Phelsuma*) don't want much light, while plants must have relatively high light intensities to survive. If you have a vertical custom-made terrarium you probably will be able to grow pothos and similar climbing vines that are enjoyed by geckos and look natural to the casual viewer. Always keep plants in their pots so you can switch them for other plants on a regular basis (about every two weeks) and give them a few days of real sunlight and natural air movement. Pots can be hidden in the substrate or under pieces of cork.

Frankly, though plants look great, they are not really seen by the geckos and may be more work than they are worth in a small terrarium. Excellent quality artificial plants are readily available to fit any habitat. Once just gaudy looking cheap copies of nature, today's artificials look better than most living plants and are sturdy enough to support the weight of a pair of rampaging geckos intent on mating. Artificials should be able to

It is important to have the terrarium completely furnished before purchasing a gecko. This enables you to have a good home all ready when the new pet arrives. This is a Madagascar Giant Day Gecko, *Phelsuma madagascariensis grandis*. Photo by I. Francais.

survive repeated soaking in a bleach solution. If cost is a factor, however, you will find that artificial plants are more expensive today than are many living plants.

The only other decorations you need are a few shallow plastic or crockery dishes for food and water. Though most geckos drink by licking water droplets off leaves and the sides of the terrarium, some actually will drink from a dish on occasion. Water dishes should have broad bases and not be over an inch deep. Shallow food dishes help confine waxworms and mealworms for a few minutes while the geckos find their prey, preventing their escape into the substrate. A narrower glass about 3 inches deep will hold small crickets while climbing geckos find their food.

It helps to have a spray bottle or two around filled with clean water at room temperature. Most gecko terraria should be lightly misted every day or two (more often for species from humid tropical habitats), making sure most of the droplets land on leaves, the glass, or decorations so they can be licked by geckos that get their water this way.

CLEANING

All lizards and other reptiles carry many types of bacteria in their intestines as part of the flora that aids their digestion—we also carry such bacteria, and so do all other animals. Unfortunately, some lizards carry bacteria of the genera *Salmonella* and *Arizona*, which can cause diarrhea, vomiting, fever, and sometimes more serious symptoms in children and adults with weak immune systems. This condition, called by the general name salmonellosis (basically a type of food poisoning), has received much negative attention of late and cannot be ignored. Since your gecko terrarium will require regular cleaning, it is not hard to modify your routine a bit to also reduce the chances of salmonellosis.

First, handle your pet as little as possible and wash your hands both before and after touching the gecko or the inside of the terrarium. Bacteria are easily transferred on dirty hands. Allow children to handle geckos only with supervision, and be sure that they keep their hands out of their mouths and do not kiss the

If you must handle your gecko, be careful of breaking off its tail or tearing its skin. The skin of day geckos, like this Madagascar Giant Day Gecko, *Phelsuma madagascariensis grandis*, is particularly fragile. Photo by I. Francais.

lizards. Soap and hot water will kill most bacteria.

Second, every week be sure that everything movable in the terrarium is soaked in a solution of bleach and hot water for at least half an hour, preferably two hours. The solution should be slightly yellowish and smell of chlorine. More expensive and complicated disinfecting chemicals are available, but household chlorine bleach *with no additives* works as well and is cheap, so you are more likely to use it strong and often. If you put the bleach solution in a bucket, you can just dump in all the dishes, cork, hiding places, plastic plants, and other movable decorations, replace them with clean ones from last week's disinfection, and then let everything sit in the bleach for a few days before rinsing in hot water and letting them dry. Disposable plastic gloves make cleaning more enjoyable and safer; bleach in small cuts and broken cuticles is not especially pleasant.

Scrub the walls of the terrarium as well, removing any feces on the glass (climbing geckos love to

Heatrocks and heatpads are just two of the many heating devices sold at pet stores. Photo: courtesy of Tetra/Second Nature.

defecate where they cling to the glass). Of course you should have been picking out feces from the substrate every day (use a plastic spoon that is cleaned or replaced often) and looking for dead food items as well. The substrate should be replaced every month or two, depending on the conditions in the terrarium—desert geckos are cleaner than tree-dwellers, and sand does not permit many bacteria and fungi to grow. If the tank ever smells sour, it is past time to change all the substrate. Most substrates are cheap, so trying to clean and reuse them is a waste of time unless you are on a really tight budget.

HEAT AND LIGHT

Most common geckos do well at room temperatures (72 to perhaps 80°F) and need little light. This is one factor that makes them easy pets that fit well into a budget—you need little in the way of expensive and complicated heaters and light units. Most geckos actually avoid warm basking areas with incandescent lights above them, but many (such as Leopard Geckos and Tokays) learn to accept a broad-spectrum fluorescent light over the terrarium. Most of the year the light can be kept on for 12 to 14 hours a day, including feeding time. Leopards seem to enjoy basking in weak light and look their best and brightest then. Weak light also aid air circulation in the terrarium, the temperature difference causing warm air to circulate through the tank.

If you feel that you need extra heat in the terrarium, it probably is best supplied with a small undertank heating pad positioned at one end of the terrarium. Never cover the entire bottom of the terrarium with a heater, as geckos usually prefer their retreats (burrows, scrapes under cork pieces, etc.) to be cooler than the warmest part of the terrarium. Always provide a temperature gradient, from a warmer end of the terrarium to a cooler end.

FEEDING

Most geckos are insectivores that also accept some plant juices. Almost all will feed on crickets of the appropriate size (not much longer than the width of the gecko's mouth). This is fortunate, because today crickets of all sizes are the most easily purchased live food for reptiles— almost every pet shop that stocks reptiles also offers crickets. Though crickets can be bred, they are slow breeders and colonies often fail in the small quarters available for them in the typical reptile room. Dealers supply a variety of sizes, from pinheads (the very smallest, suitable for hatchlings and adults of tiny species) to 10-day-olds (about 0.12 inch long and excellent for small species), on through those 0.25, 0.5, and 0.75 inch to full adults an inch long. Purchase 500 or a thousand crickets at a time

for the lowest cost and store them in a deep plastic tub or old aquarium with a shallow sand layer on the bottom and a very shallow water dish filled with cotton or a piece of sponge (crickets seem to have a suicidal instinct to drown in any water container). Feed them on cereals, green leafy vegetables, grated carrots or apple slices (beware the growth of fungus), or specially vitamin-supplemented commercial cricket foods.

Before feeding, some keepers prefer to cut (not pull) the hind legs off larger crickets to make them easier to catch and eat. (This may be considered cruel by some and may actually be illegal in some areas.) There is no controversy about the fact that crickets must be given supplemental vitamins and calcium before being fed, however. Insects contain much more phosphorus than calcium in their tissues, and thus a natural insect is not always a great food for a gecko, especially if it has been held in captivity for several days or weeks and fed a monotonous diet of oatmeal or bran and lettuce. Calcium and vitamin supplements made especially for reptiles are cheap and readily available at your pet shop. They should be added to all food fed to the crickets the day before they become prey for the geckos, a process called gut-loading. The supplements are still in the intestines of the crickets when they are eaten by the geckos and the prey thus serves to transmit essential calcium and vitamins to the gecko. Alternatively, a finely powdered supplement is placed in a small plastic bag, a few crickets are added, the neck of the bag is twisted shut, and the contents are lightly shaken to get the supplement on the crickets. This is the "shake and bake" method. Supplements adhere better if the case of waxworms. Like other insects, they contain a much higher proportion of phosphorus to calcium than is healthy for a gecko, so they are treated much like crickets, with supplements added to the food of the mealworms and both types of food going through the shake and bake

Adult Leopard Geckos, *Eublepharis macularius*, and other large geckos can occasionally be given pink mice. They make a good addition to a well-rounded diet. Photo by J. Merli.

crickets are slightly moist, but moist crickets also attract fine sand and may lead to gut impactions in small geckos. Dry crickets are better.

Other readily available foods for geckos are mealworms and waxworms. Both are larvae of insects, a flour beetle in the case of mealworms and a moth in the technique before being fed. Some keepers inject liquid supplements into the bodies of the worms. Mealworms and waxworms are best thought of as treats given perhaps once a week rather than the every other day feeding of crickets.

Two cautions with these foods are necessary. Both crickets and mealworms have strong jaws and in theory could eat their way into or out of a small gecko. Large numbers of adult crickets should not be left for long periods with small geckos. We lost a gravid Turkish Gecko to crickets in just one day—her sluggish condition before laying apparently allowed the crickets to attack and eat three holes in her sides and belly;

waxworms (special mixes based on honey and oatmeal are available as food), be sure that none escape—we have had cultures of waxworms that literally were "waxworms from hell," eating through plastic sheets, cardboard, and supposedly insect-proof containers to escape and become pests for months.

Although mealworms are not a good staple food, they are useful components in a varied diet. They are also very easy to raise. Photo by W. P. Mara.

she died a day later. There are repeated stories of large mealworms literally eating through the gut of a small lizard and exiting alive through the belly. Large mealworms should be killed by crushing the head, dipping them in hot water, or slitting them open with small scissors so the thick cuticle does not prevent the gecko's digestive juices from dissolving the mealworm. The second problem is that if you attempt to rear

Fruitflies are excellent food for hatchlings and small adults. They are readily purchased from specialist dealers, often in kit form that allows you to rear several generations before the colony becomes overwhelmed with fungus. Wild-caught insects are excellent treats for many geckos, especially as they contain a variety of essential vitamins that may be absent from cultured insects and also may have a calcium to phosphorus ratio

Prey insects should usually be smaller than the gecko's head. Adult Leopard Geckos, *Eublepharis macularius*, however, can manage fairly large insects, like this grasshopper. Photo by M. Gilroy.

nearer the one to one needed by geckos. All insects should be collected from areas that are not treated with pesticides, insecticides, herbicides, or other -icides, which may be deadly to small lizards. Insect nets work well to sweep small insects from shrubs and weeds, while "pooters"(aspirators) are used to suck even tinier insects from flowers. Some geckos will take pillbugs as treats; these are found under rotting logs and other debris and can be stored for a week or more in a small plastic margarine tub with some leaf litter from their natural habitat. Pinkie mice are taken by many large geckos and provide an excellent source of calcium from the skeleton.

Don't neglect plant juices from the diet of your geckos. Madagascar day geckos (*Phelsuma*) are well-known for feeding on nectar and honey, but many other geckos, even Leopards, will take occasional treats of a 50-50 mix of water and honey served in a small plastic cup. Calcium and vitamins can be added to the mix, especially when served to gravid females that need extra calcium for their eggs. Strained peach and mango baby food is taken by many geckos, not just the *Phelsuma* species. These semiliquid foods can be served in small plastic cups (bottlecaps work well) or even in walnut shells if you like a more natural look. Because they contain so much sugar, they should not be allowed to sit in the terrarium for more than a day.

Try to provide as much variety for your geckos as possible and feed on a regular schedule. Commonly crickets are fed every other day, with a meal of waxworms or small mealworms on the weekend. Honey water or baby food might be given twice a week for most species, of course more often for those that need lots of nectar substitutes in their diet. If you have gravid females, it won't hurt to provide a small dish of calcium supplement or even powdered cuttlebone, which may be eaten directly by the gecko.

BREEDING

The following is a very general treatment of breeding geckos, and obviously more specialized knowledge is necessary for most species. Treat all the following comments with the prefix "as a general rule" and remember to check for more detailed information later in the book.

Male geckos generally are larger than females and have distinct bulges at the base of the tail to house the copulatory organs, the hemipenes. They also often have distinct pores in front of the cloaca (pre-anal pores) or under the hind legs (femoral pores) that are smaller or absent in females. Many male geckos call when ready to breed, either to mark their territory or perhaps to attract females.

A typical breeding colony can consist of one male and one to three females. Using several females to one male may lengthen the life of a female, since matings will occur less often and she will spend less time gravid. Producing eggs puts a great strain on a female's metabolism. Never put two male geckos in one

A humidified shelter can double as a nesting box if you are interested in breeding your geckos. Leopard Geckos, *Eublepharis macularius*, will readily breed if given the proper conditions. Photo by I. Francais.

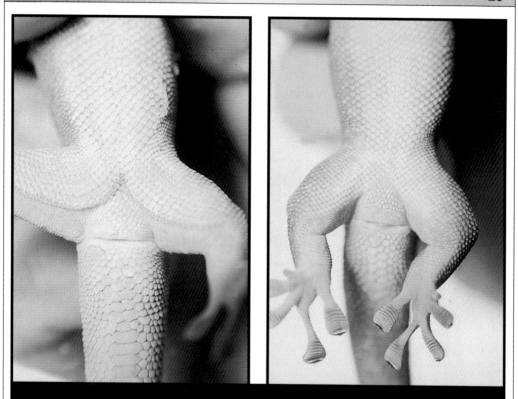

Some species of geckos are easier to sex than others. The Madagascar Giant Day Gecko, *Phelsuma madagascariensis grandis*, is relatively easy, at least if you look at adults. Left: This individual has well-developed pores on the thighs and before the vent. Thus, it is a male. Right: The pores on this one are nearly invisible, so it is a female. Photo by I. Francais.

terrarium—there will be fighting over territory and females, and one male may be injured or even killed. Mating may be rough, with males running down females and holding on to their necks with the teeth. Many females end the mating season with torn skin on the neck and small infections, but if they are healthy they rapidly recover.

Once you notice that a female is gravid (the eggs often are visible through the belly skin and their large size gives a female a distinctive bulky appearance), she must be provided with a proper place to lay her eggs. Most eyelid geckos like a plastic box (such as a sandwich box) with a tight lid and a hole cut into the side. The box is nearly filled with vermiculite that is kept moist but not wet and checked daily. Typical geckos usually want to place their eggs in a crevice between layers of wood or rock, though many will use a vermiculite-filled nesting box as well.

Geckos lay two types of eggs. Eyelid geckos lay elongated or oval eggs of large size with flexible shells that readily absorb water from the environment. (Diplodactylins, including the giant geckos, also lay flexible eggs.) Such eggs should be incubated in moist vermiculite. Most geckos lay spherical to slightly oval hard-shelled eggs that stick to crevices in bark or rocks and may be almost impossible to safely remove. If the eggs cannot be removed to a vermiculite incubator box, they can be covered with a small cup containing a bit of moist sphagnum; the cup is taped directly over the eggs, but not touching them.

Virtually all geckos lay two eggs per clutch, and most lay three or four clutches per season. Incubation times and temperatures vary greatly, but most will hatch in 60 to 90 days if kept at 82 to 85°F. Hatchlings are active immediately after leaving the shell, something to remember when providing a lid for the incubator holding climbing gecko eggs. They take their first meal within a week, after their first shed. Geckos grow fast, and within a few months they probably will be indistinguishable from the adults. They may be sexually mature in eight to ten months. Hatchlings should not be kept with adults, as they may be treated as normal prey and

Vermiculite is probably the most widely used substrate for incubating reptile eggs. It holds moisture and resists mold and fungus. These are hatching Leopard Gecko eggs, *Eublepharis macularius*. Photo by Isabelle Francais.

grabbed as they go by. Almost all hatchling geckos drink by lapping water droplets from the plants or walls of the terrarium.

Remember that you do not have to breed your pets if you don't want to. Though there is much talk about saving species through captive breeding, there are enough commercial breeders of all the common gecko species to supply the market for several years. Additionally, consider what you will do with your young if you get them—will you be able to house and feed them, or will you have to try to find them a home? The market for most common geckos is saturated and you will not be able to sell ordinary specimens (uncommon species and unusual color varieties are of course more salable). Crickets are expensive and large gecko colonies take a lot of time to maintain. Don't be stampeded into breeding just to prove that you can do it.

Geckos typically lay two large eggs, just as this Leopard Gecko has done. It is usually safest to remove the eggs from the terrarium to an incubator. Photo by I. Francais.

THE EYELIDS HAVE IT

LEOPARD GECKOS AND ALLIES
Without a doubt, the best geckos for the beginning keeper are the Leopard Gecko, *Eublepharis macularius*, from western India and Pakistan, and the Fat-tailed Gecko, *Hemitheconyx caudicinctus*, of tropical western Africa. These two species have the large size (usually 8 inches in large males) and placid temperament necessary to make a good pet. Though they do not always appreciate handling, certainly many Leopard Geckos tolerate careful stroking, and some seem to enjoy it.

These and some other 16 species comprise the family Eublepharidae, most readily recognized by the presence of movable eyelids, thus the common name eyelid geckos. All the species are terrestrial or nearly so (the cat geckos, *Aeluroscalabotes*, climb to some degree) without strongly developed climbing pads under the fingers and toes. Three genera are commonly seen in the terrarium hobby.

Cat geckos, like this *Aeluroscalabotes felinus*, are rarely seen eyelid geckos. They come from Thailand and other parts of southeast Asia. Photo by P. Freed

Leopard Geckos breed very well in captivity. The current trend is to selectively breed for interesting colors and patterns, like this leucistic morph. Photo by P. Freed.

THE LEOPARD GECKO

Every hobbyist has seen a Leopard Gecko, *Eublepharis macularius*, in the pet shop. This gecko is bred in very large numbers each year and is the least expensive captive-bred gecko. It is a sturdy species, with a large head, large eyes, rather small but strong legs, and a large, thick tail that seldom is dropped and usually is the original unless a bad accident has happened. The scales of the back are small, with scattered larger tubercles in more or less regular rows. The iris of the eye is heavily reticulated with grayish silvery, and the pupil is a plain vertical slit with bright golden edges. Typical adults are light to dark yellow with few to many irregular dark brown spots, often with pale purplish shading between them. The head has dark brown spots on top and often a stripe from the eye to nostril, the upper lip with or without spotting but never bright white. Adults are about 6 to 8 inches long, the males usually larger and with broader heads than the females. Males also have a row of distinct pre-anal pores in front of the cloaca.

Hatchlings begin life with a very different pattern. The 3-inch lizards are pale yellow with about three broad blackish brown bands over the back, the top of the head solid blackish brown or nearly so, and the tail strongly banded in blackish and white. There is a distinct nuchal loop, a pale curved band behind the head extending along the upper jaws. Many captive-bred

Leopards have all the dark pattern strongly purple-tinged, with the top of the head spotted almost from hatching. There usually is a bright blue area over each eye, actually the membranes of the eye itself showing through translucent skin. With growth this pattern slowly breaks up into irregular lines and spots connected by

females (young or adult) will be happy in a 10-gallon terrarium with an inch or two of fine playbox sand in the bottom. They do well at 75 to 85°F and thus do not need supplemental heating in most situations. If you decide that their terrarium will become too cool, use a small heating pad under one side of the tank for best results. Some

Attractive color, docile temperament, and an endearing face have made the Leopard Gecko one of the most popular of all lizards. Photo by M. Bacon.

pale purplish brown bands, the spotting becoming more distinct while the purplish becomes weaker. Eventually (about one to two years) the fully spotted adult pattern develops. Sexual maturity is reached at about one to two years of age, though we have had specimens less than a year old lay eggs.

Keeping Leopards is simplicity itself. A trio of one male and two

hobbyists suggest a winter cooling to about 65 to 75°F for best chances of breeding next spring, but this is not necessary with captive-bred specimens from established lines that have become adapted to captivity. In many respects Leopard Geckos are domesticated animals, and there is no reason today to ever purchase a wild-caught specimen. Captive-breds almost

This Leopard Gecko has reduced spotting and is mostly yellow. Individuals that have been bred for these aberrant markings are more expensive than normal ones. Photo by I. Francais.

always eat well (crickets, waxworms, mealworms, other insects, with an occasional pinkie mouse and a weekly cup of honey water mix or fruit baby food) and are healthy.

Though in theory nocturnal, most specimens seem to like a weak light over the terrarium and will bask under broad-spectrum fluorescent lights. Most enjoy handling (Careful! Rough handling can tear the skin or even cause the tail to be dropped!) and seldom bite. The pinch of a large male can be painful but probably won't draw blood.

Though Leopards are rather sluggish, they can move when they want to. When stalking crickets they stare at their prey, become stiff-legged, and tend to swish the tail from side to side much like a cat. (Similar tail swishing is common in many geckos.) They soon learn their feeding schedule and will start trying to climb the glass if the keeper comes near on feeding night. Pets feed heavily and also shed heavily. Shedding is a fascinating process to watch. The gecko turns dull grayish two or three days before shedding. When ready to shed, the Leopard rubs the snout and lips against a rough surface to start loosening the skin. A Leopard Gecko eats its old skin as it sheds, actually reaching around to pull off large chunks and then chowing it down. There should be no patches of skin left on the body after a good shed. (A daily misting with

Leopard Geckos, *Eublepharis macularius*, usually exhibit a good disposition. In fact, they are one of the best lizards to purchase if you want a lizard that will tolerate handling. Photo by I. Francais.

Although not frequently seen in pet stores, the banded geckos, like this Big Bend Gecko, *Coleonyx reticulatus*, make hardy and interesting captives. Photo by K. H. Switak.

room-temperature water helps assure proper humidity.) Occasionally a nearly complete shed skin will be found in the terrarium, probably from a young specimen or a very well-fed adult that just isn't hungry enough to bother eating its skin.

Most of a Leopard's day is spent under cover (we have lots of luck with curved pieces of cork bark) or basking on top of the cork when the lights are turned on. Fourteen hours of light per day most of the year, reduced to ten during the winter, works well. Our specimens have shown no inclination to burrow, though in nature they occupy burrows in bleak stony and sandy desert areas of western India and Pakistan, an area noted for hot summers and cold winters. Perhaps pet Leopards are just "happy" to be in a stable terrarium with regular meals. Well-kept pets may live ten years.

As with most other geckos, mating is rough, with the male chasing down the female, holding her in his mouth by the nape of the neck, and twisting their bodies around so the cloacas are in contact. Actual copulation is short and not often seen. In about five weeks a gravid female begins to appear excessively plump, and you may be able to see the outlines of two large elongated eggs through the skin of her whitish belly. At this time she may begin to bask more often, staying in the warmest part of the terrarium, and might take calcium supplement from a small cup. Be sure to increase the calcium supplementation on her crickets and added to the honey or baby food. Also provide a vermiculite-filled laying box. Keep it at least half filled with damp vermiculite and check it each day. She may or may not lay in the box (some females seem to be very stubborn about finding the proper laying place and eventually just give up and drop the eggs anywhere), so check each day for eggs in corners or under the hiding spots. The first eggs are laid about six weeks after mating. A single large female may lay two eggs every month for four months in a row. Younger females tend to lay only one or two rather irregular eggs perhaps twice per season.

As soon as you find an egg, mark the upper surface with a dot from a felt-tip pen and move it to an incubator. Sex in

Hatchling Leopard Geckos are often nervous and skittish. If you are patient, they will quickly settle down and become docile pets. Photo by M. Gilroy.

Telling a hatchling Leopard Gecko from a hatchling Fat-tailed Gecko, *Hemitheconyx caudicinctus*, is not easy. Baby Leopard Geckos have a white crescent mark behind the head. This lizard is a Fat-tailed Gecko, and, thus, has no such mark. Photo by P. Freed.

Leopards is determined by the temperature at which the eggs are incubated, not by genetics. As a rule, more females are produced at lower temperatures (80 to 84°F), while more males are produced at higher temperatures (86 to 90°F), with both sexes at median temperatures. (Temperatures over 90°F produce mostly females again, but very few eggs hatch at such high temperatures.) The eggs must be kept moderately moist during incubation and will hatch in as little as six weeks or as much as ten weeks. The 3-inch (rarely to 4 inches) hatchlings use stored yolk for

their first week then shed their skin and take tiny crickets.

As more and more Leopard Geckos have been bred, color varieties have developed, including a nearly solid yellow lutino that is said to be genetic but might also be produced by unusual incubation conditions. Albinos are known, as are very dark, nearly melanistic animals. Adults with stripes rather than spots have been produced. Breeders have been selecting their lines for bright colors with reduced dark spotting for many generations, and few captive-bred adults have the many dark irregular spots of wild adults. If you take photos of your pets at regular intervals from hatchling to adulthood, you can follow changes in the pattern and perhaps even predict how the pattern will change with the next shed. The pattern of spots on the head and body is very specific and often can be used to identify individuals through most of their lives.

This is the number one gecko for the beginner, the commercial breeder, and the advanced hobbyist interested in producing color varieties. They also are simply great pets.

THE FAT-TAILED GECKO

The other major eyelid gecko is the Fat-tail, *Hemitheconyx caudicinctus*, an 8-inch (rarely 10 inches) species from western Africa. This is not a species of the rain forests, however, preferring to burrow in drier areas on sunny hillsides and at the edges of the savanna. Their burrows may be relatively moist, and this species definitely likes it more humid than the Leopard. In captivity we've had good luck keeping Fat-tails on a bed of vermiculite that is kept just barely moist, along with regular mistings. They are nocturnal and less likely to be seen during the day than are Leopards, spending most of their time in hiding. They are a bit touchier than Leopards and more likely to bite, but they generally do not resent handling and may even enjoy being picked up. The only nipping problem we've had was when a juvenile was wedged in a hollow piece of cholla branch (the whitish wood that looks like a piece of fish netting) and objected to being removed. They like temperatures a bit higher than Leopards, in the 85 to 92°F range, but captive-bred specimens seem to be more adaptable to lower temperatures, and we have kept them at room temperatures with no extra heating and had good luck. Like Leopards, they may bask under weak fluorescent lighting, but this does not appear to be necessary.

A Fat-tailed Gecko is an impressive sight. This is a very heavily built gecko with a broad head and a very thick tail (storing fat for emergencies) that is circled by rings of raised scales. Adults and juveniles have a similar pattern. The top of the head is uniformly brown, there is a very wide tan to yellow nuchal loop that extends forward to under the eye, and there are two broad brown bands on the back. In adults the brown areas are outlined with white and may appear scalloped or irregular around the edges. The tail also is banded with brown. There is much variation in background color. Wild specimens are pale tan to pale brown, with the dark brown bands not always well-defined. Captive-bred geckos have been selectively bred for brighter colors, and many have bright orange, yellow, or pinkish tan backgrounds against very dark brown bands, resulting in high-contrast animals. In nature some 10 to 15% of Fat-tails have a white stripe down the center of the back from the top of the head to the tail. Captive-bred striped geckos may have the band very wide and shiny white to tinged with orange. It has been said that mating striped to striped produces striped animals, while mating striped to normal produces a percentage of striped animals, but little has been published on the genetics of the Fat-tail.

Until recently few Fat-tails bred in captivity, but the breakthrough occurred about five years ago, and today many captive-breds are available at reasonable cost (though usually much more than the cost of Leopards). Males tend to be larger than females (though not always) and are recognized by the broader head, presence of

Captive-bred Fat-tailed Geckos, *Hemitheconyx caudicinctus*, have recently become more available. The hobby may soon see some interesting color varieties produced by breeders. Photo by I. Francais.

Fat-tails must be kept a bit warmer and more humid than Leopards, but otherwise they are very similar. They feed on a variety of insects, especially crickets, and also take occasional treats of honey water and baby food. They can be kept as trios of one male and two females in a 10-gallon terrarium.

pre-anal pores, and thickened tail base. Mating takes place as in the Leopard Gecko, but so far occurs mostly in the winter months, especially November. There may be a rough and tumble mating chase followed by wrestling between the sexes. Some breeders recommend keeping the male separate from the female all year, putting the sexes together only during November, but there is little evidence either way so far. Eggs may be visible in the female in just three weeks, and you must be sure to provide a laying box filled with moist vermiculite.

Incubation of the two elongated, soft-shelled eggs takes some 7 to 88°F, while temperatures between 84 and 86°F produce both sexes. Hatchlings are rather small, usually under 3 inches, and active from the beginning. Each must be given its own hiding spot and kept moist through daily misting. Feeding begins after the first shed, usually less than a week after hatching. They may be

The attractive striped morph of the Fat-tailed Gecko seems to be more popular than the normal color. This dull-colored individual looks like it's ready to shed. Photo by I. Francais.

12 weeks. The eggs should be kept moist and at somewhat higher average temperatures than in Leopards. Like Leopards, the sexes are determined by incubation temperature. Below 84°F you will get mostly females, and the same is true at 93 or 94°F; males are produced at 86 to sexually mature in just a year and are best bred when 18 months old.

The Fat-tailed Gecko has already found a spot in the terrarium hobby and is sure to become increasingly popular as prices drop, more captive-breds become available, and the colors become more brilliant through selective breeding. Albinos have been bred. Though not yet as hardy or long-lived as Leopards (expect a lifetime of seven or eight years), their large size and complacent nature make them great pets. In many specimens the lips have a tendency to curl upward a bit at the back, producing a rather odd and sardonic smile that is unique and appealing. How can anyone ignore a pet that smiles back at you when you feed it?

BANDED GECKOS

The genus *Coleonyx* is a strictly American group of eyelid geckos found in deserts and other dry habitats from central Texas to southern California and then south over Mexico into Central America. Currently some seven species are recognized, three with subspecies, and they are not always easy to identify to the species level. Three species occur in the United States, with the other four species found only in Mexico and Central America. As a rule, they are smaller (seldom over 6 inches in adult females, which are larger than males in this genus), more slender geckos than the Leopard or Fat-tail, and they tend to have a pattern of several brown bands across the back coupled with a narrow whitish to yellowish nuchal loop. (One species, *C. switaki*, is spotted and one, *C. reticulatus*, has a greatly reduced dark pattern, however.) Males tend to have larger, wider, more rounded heads than females of similar size and age and also have more pointed, longer spurs on either side of the cloaca, as well as large bulges at the base of the tail to house the hemipenes. They lack climbing pads under the fingers and toes and thus cannot climb the glass of a terrarium, making escapes unlikely. Three species appear in the terrarium with some regularity.

The Western Banded Gecko, *Coleonyx variegatus*, is a common nocturnal species found from western New Mexico to California and into northern Mexico. Adults seldom exceed 5 inches in total length and are pale yellowish tan above, white below, usually with a pattern of five or six broad dark brown bands across the back and many more bands on the tail. There are several subspecies that differ somewhat in color pattern and adult size, and in some the adult pattern is greatly broken up and looks like a mix of spots and a brown network. These little geckos may be very common in dry habitats, spending the day under rocks, fallen cacti, and in shallow burrows but emerging at night to feed on beetles and a variety of other insects and invertebrates. They adapt well to man and often remain common at the edges of cities. In fact, our first Western Banded Geckos were rescued from a relative's cat. Each night the cat went hunting behind the house near Tucson and brought back a variety of small lizards and even snakes as "gifts." The two we rescued had lost their tails and were of course frightened, but they calmed down

Because of their hardiness and small size, Texas Banded Geckos, *Coleonyx brevis*, make ideal choices for a naturalistic desert terrarium. Photo by K. H. Switak.

in a day or so and accepted small crickets. The tails were regenerated within six weeks, and the geckos still seem none the worst for wear.

These lizards like a dry, quiet, dark terrarium with a good bit of cover such as pieces of cork bark. They do well at room temperature but also tolerate short periods of up to 94°F. (Contrary to popular opinion, most desert animals like it cool, not hot; they hide during the day in cooler burrows and only emerge when temperatures drop at night.) A daily spraying provides them with sufficient water. They are delicate geckos that do not like to be handled and will drop their tails readily when disturbed, so leave them alone except when cleaning the cage. They take a variety of small insects, including the usual crickets.

Females lay two soft-shelled eggs at a time and may produce three or four clutches each summer. They should be incubated like a Leopard Gecko's eggs at about 78 to 86°F. Unlike the Leopard and Fat-tail, sex in the banded geckos is genetically determined and not affected by temperature. Incubation usually takes six to ten weeks, producing hatchlings only 2 inches long that require tiny insects such as fruitflies and pinhead crickets.

The Texas Banded Gecko, *Coleonyx brevis*, is very similar to the Western Banded Gecko but is somewhat smaller and often even more slender. Many specimens are taken each spring in Texas (the species ranges over much of central and western Texas plus adjacent New Mexico and Mexico) and reach the terrarium market, but it is not commonly available as captive-bred specimens. The best way to tell it from the Western Banded Gecko is to look at the pre-anal pores (present in both sexes in this genus): in *brevis* there are six or fewer pores that form a line broken in the center; in *variegatus* there are six to ten pores that form a more complete line. The Texas Banded Gecko can be kept much like the Western Banded but is even more delicate to handle.

Typical of the Central American banded geckos is *Coleonyx mitratus*, a 6- to 7-inch species from somewhat more humid habitats than the northern species. It is best kept in a small terrarium on a substrate of soil and peat moss that offers a constant humidity supplemented by daily misting. Water is licked from plants and the sides of the terrarium, so there is no need for a water dish. If kept at about 80°F, they feed well on crickets and even may breed in captivity. Females may produce a clutch of two eggs every three weeks most of the year, though this certainly will not lead to a long life for the female. The eggs hatch in about eight to ten weeks if incubated at 82°F. The hatchlings are little gems, mostly brown with narrow yellow bands edged with black. With growth the bands tend to break up into spots and irregular stripes. Sexual maturity is reached in as little as six months, but they should not be bred until nearly a year old.

Because of their small size and delicate nature that does not promote handling, banded geckos perhaps are not the best of pets, but they are fairly hardy and require little care, which can make them a good choice for a beginner. Unfortunately few captive-bred banded geckos are available, but this could change any day if a few breeders become interested in the group.

CALLING ALL GEKKOS

With the genus *Gekko* we come to what are perhaps the most aggressive geckos available to hobbyists. The two dozen or more species of the genus usually are called simply the tokay geckos because the genus contains the best-known of all the geckos, *Gekko gecko*, the Tokay. They also are known as the calling geckos because males on territory often have a loud and distinctive call that is part of the night sounds throughout the range of the genus, from India over southern China to Japan, then over Southeast Asia and the Indonesian islands plus the Philippines. They tend to be large and powerful lizards with wide, undivided climbing pads under all the fingers and toes. Four of the toes end in claws, while the small inner toe lacks a claw. The eyes are large and prominent, with a scalloped vertical pupil and a row of projecting scales around the edge of the eye. Scalation varies from nearly uniformly covered with fine tubercular scales to having many scattered large tubercles. Males differ from females in having larger heads and prominent pores under the hind legs and before the cloaca (the femoral and pre-anal pores, respectively).

Most species of *Gekko* are poorly known rather brownish forms, but a few species with bright color patterns are available in addition to the Tokay. All are generally similar in their requirements to the Tokay, which is perhaps one of the easiest geckos to care for, though not an especially good pet.

Give your Tokay Geckos, *Gekko gecko*, a humid terrarium and they will be healthy long-lived pets. Photo by I. Francais.

THE TOKAY GECKO

One of the most brightly colored of the geckos, this is a lizard with a reputation as a biter that just cannot be handled. *Gekko gecko* (yes, the generic and specific names are spelled differently—just a coincidence of taxonomic history) ranges from eastern India and southern China over Southeast Asia into the Philippines, Sumatra, Java, and the smaller Indonesian islands. Part of this range certainly is not natural, as the gecko often stows away in plants and cargoes of ships, letting it become more widely distributed. A species of the open forest, it is tolerant of human disturbance and gets along well in cities. Many visitors to Asian cities report that Tokays appear on porches and near street lights as soon as the sun goes down, racing across ceilings and poles in search of large moths, grasshoppers, roaches, and other tropical insects attracted to the lights. Males tend to stake out their own corners and challenge other geckos by opening the mouth to reveal the bright pink tongue and linings and yelling "to-key" repeatedly. Females occasionally croak but do not have a well-formed call.

Tokays are about 10 inches long when fully grown, with a long, rather slender tail. The feet are large, with wide pads, and the head is large and has strong jaw muscles. The eye is bright gold, and the iris has four pinholes. Coloration varies individually, with age, and perhaps geographically. Young specimens tend to be rather dark blue-gray with about seven or eight rows of round white spots across the back and distinct white bands around the tail. There are rusty red spots in rather regular rows over the back and head. With growth the background color tends to pale, the white spots become more irregular in size and arrangement, and the rusty red spots often turn bright orange and become more prominent. Some adults appear to be bright bluish gray with orange spots about half the size of the eye over the entire head, body, and legs. Others are much duller, with the red subdued against dull gray. Cold specimens tend to be dull in color, warm specimens brighter. The belly is white. There are large tubercles scattered among the scales of the back and sides, some of these bearing sharp points.

Because of their aggressive nature, Tokays are best kept individually in 10- to 20-gallon terraria that are securely covered. Provide a substrate of gravel, sand, or vermiculite and a few rocks or pieces of cork bark as resting areas during the day. They

Hatchling Tokay Geckos, *Gekko gecko*, are just as feisty and pugnacious as the adults. It is very rare for one to become a tame pet. Photo by R. D. Bartlett.

like to climb, so give them a sturdy branch and some artificial plants for security. They do well at room temperature or a bit warmer, about 77 to 86°F, with a small heating pad in one corner and a weak basking light turned on after feeding at night. Allow the temperature to drop a bit at night and be sure to spray the terrarium daily. Tokays will drink from a small water dish and also will lap droplets from the walls. They will eat anything, from adult crickets and mealworms to moths and butterflies, earthworms, and the occasional pinkie mouse. Feed Tokays heavily if you want to keep them healthy—most imports (few captive-breds are available) are emaciated from not feeding sufficiently over the week or more they were in transit. Such specimens need to be carefully watched for the development of stress-related diseases and should be allowed to eat their fill each day while kept at a humidity level of 75% or more. A large Tokay will eat a small Tokay, even if both are emaciated, so be warned and keep every lizard separately except when trying to mate them.

Like many other nocturnal geckos, Tokays have narrow vertical pupils with scalloped edges. Photo by W. P. Mara.

Mating may occur at any time of the year in captivity, and the female produces two large round eggs with thick shells. The eggs usually are stuck to a corner of the terrarium or in bark crevices and may be almost impossible to remove from their attachment site without damage. Males may guard the developing eggs and even the newly hatched young, so you may have a small fight on your hands to remove the eggs to an incubator. You might be better off just covering them with a cup of gauze. The eggs are not very sensitive to low humidity and cool temperatures, but they do best in a moderately moist incubator at about 85°F. Incubation takes three to six months (obviously depending somewhat on temperature), resulting in nearly black hatchlings with white bands. The young are almost 4 inches long at hatching and grow fast if fed heavily, becoming sexually mature in about a year.

Unfortunately Tokays have a bad bite and will draw blood if allowed to fasten to a hand or finger. They don't just pinch, but also twist and pull, increasing the pain. They move fast and can escape from a terrarium in the blinking of an eye, and they are almost impossible to catch again without a net. For a while there was a fad where apartment dwellers in New York and other large cities tried to use Tokays to control roaches. Pet shops sold many of these geckos, and for a few weeks they worked well at their purpose. However, Tokays cannot stand the cool winter temperatures and low humidities of New York apartments and also are very subject to insecticide residues in the roaches. Some apartment residents also complained of the loud calls keeping them awake at night and did not appreciate the large amounts of gecko droppings that tended to accumulate under the Tokay's favored corner.

OTHER TOKAYS

With over two dozen species, it is not surprising that several other *Gekko* species occasionally reach the pet shops. Few of these are seen in any abundance and few have been bred in captivity with any regularity. Most tokays are brownish gray above with white spots in various arrangements on the back and sometimes a narrow pale stripe down the center of the back. Three species are more colorful, however, and have gained a small following in the hobby.

Green-eyed Geckos, *Gekko smithi*, are rarely seen in herpetoculture. They should be kept in the same conditions as the Tokay Gecko, *Gekko gecko*. Photo by R. G. Sprackland.

The Green-eyed Gecko, **Gekko smithi**, is found from Burma and Thailand south over Indonesia. Several species were included under this name until recently, and it is not always possible to distinguish them externally. As used in the broad sense, *Gekko smithi* is readily recognized by the combination of large body size (males often over 10 inches long, females about 10% shorter), rows of white spots across the greenish to brown back lacking red spots, and a bright green iris. Specimens from the Indonesian islands are the true *G. smithi*, with 8 to 14 rows of large tubercular scales across the back at midbody and often a greenish coloration. Specimens of Green-eyed Geckos imported from Thailand probably

belong to the recently described **G. taylori**, which has 16 to 19 rows of tubercles and often a dark brownish coloration. The name *G. stentor* sometimes used for the Green-eyed Gecko is a synonym of true *smithi*.

Attractive but uncommon, White-striped Geckos, *Gekko vittatus*, are usually only available as wild-caught individuals. Photo by K. H. Switak.

The White-striped Gecko, **Gekko vittatus,** is another large tokay from southern Asia. Adults are distinctively patterned, being dark brown to greenish brown above and on the sides, with a clean white stripe running from the nape to the anterior tail. At the front the line splits to form a Y with the branches ending at the eyes, while on the tail the stripe ends suddenly as a slightly widened area; the posterior part of the tail may be mostly whitish or just brown with large white spots. It can be treated much like the true Tokay.

The Golden Gecko, **Gekko ulikovski**, was described just in 1993 and has been imported in large numbers from Vietnam over the last few years. It is a large, rather slender tokay that is dark olive-green or greenish brown over

The White-striped Gecko, *Gekko vittatus*, is sometimes sold under the names Striped Gecko and Skunk Gecko. Photo by M. Panzella.

the back and sides without a well-defined pattern. However, its claim to fame is a large patch of bright to subdued golden yellow from the back of the head over the middle of the back that gives it a unique appearance. The center of the belly also may be bright yellow. Ours have been kept much like true Tokays, at a warm room temperature with daily misting, and eat like hogs. All the specimens we've seen so far have been imports, often in bad condition, emaciated, stressed, with missing tails, torn skin, and sometimes missing toes. Choose your specimens carefully, keep an eye out for mite infestations (which can be treated with chemicals from your pet store), and feed them heavily. It can be assumed that they will breed much like the Tokay, but so far males have not been present in the ones we've examined.

Other tokays appear on occasion, but they probably have little to offer the beginning hobbyist and are of more interest to specialists. One of these is the Butterfly Gecko, ***Gekko monarchus***, an 8-inch species from Thailand south through the Indonesian islands and the Philippines. It is a brownish species shaped much like a normal Tokay but with a distinctive pattern of about ten pairs of small black spots on either side of the back, these often separated by a narrow pale stripe and vaguely resembling the spread wings of a butterfly. The spots continue onto the tail to form dark rings. Once imported fairly commonly, it has been displaced because of lack of bright colors but still makes a decent pet if you can take a large, aggressive gecko. The pair of large hard-shelled eggs hatch in about three months. Sexes may be hard to distinguish as both males and females have pre-anal pores, though those of the female are small and poorly developed.

Because of their fluctuating availability and uncertain population levels, keepers of the beautiful Golden Gecko, *Gekko ulikovski*, would be wise to breed them. Photo by R. D. Bartlett.

A FEW BROWN GECKOS

It's likely that if you were to look up all the gecko species, most would be just dull brown and tan lizards without striking colors or other features. This simplicity of color does not mean that they would make poor pets, just not conspicuous ones. Here we'll quickly discuss four genera of little (or big in a couple of cases) brown geckos with good terrarium potential that should not be ignored just because they are not brightly colored.

Although mostly brown, Madagascan Big-head Geckos, *Paroedura pictus*, still have an attractive pattern. They are hardy, but seem to have a short life span. Photo by M. Burger.

MADAGASCAN BIG-HEADS

Known by many common names, *Paroedura pictus* is a small (under 6 inches) species found in the dry forests of Madagascar. Once considered part of the gigantic genus *Phyllodactylus*, it differs in small features of the skeleton, but hobbyists can easily recognize it by the lack of distinct climbing pads under the fingers and toes (juveniles have two leaf-like pads that are hard to see in adults) and the oversized head that somehow seems out of proportion to the rather chunky body. The skin of the head is fused to the bones beneath, and the body is covered with fairly regular rows of large tubercles separated by the usual tiny scales. There is a striped phase and a banded phase, and each may have darker and lighter individuals. Banded individuals are reddish brown with about five narrow angled white bands over the back, each outlined in darker brown. The striped phase has the bands broken at the center of the back by a broad white to yellow stripe outlined with dark brown; the stripe runs from the back of the head onto the tail. The tail is spotted or mottled with reddish brown and has many rather pointed tubercles.

Their small size and lack of climbing ability (they can climb on plants but not on glass once they are half grown) make them easy to house, with a male and two or three females keepable in a 10-gallon terrarium. The substrate should be fairly dry, of sand or wood chips, and there should be hiding places provided. Mist the terrarium daily and provide a somewhat more moist area (a plastic box is fine) containing sphagnum to assure easy shedding and a place for females to lay their eggs. They can be kept at room temperature but like it a bit warmer, perhaps 82 to as much as 90°F. Though nocturnal, they readily adjust to weak lighting and may bask in the glow of a broad-spectrum fluorescent fixture.

Big-heads feed on the usual array of crickets and other insects and will take water from a dish as well as lapping droplets from the walls. This species appears to enjoy chasing down pillbugs, stalking them with intense concentration and the slender tail held curled over the back like a scorpion's tail. Provide the usual honey water and baby food treats and supplements. Females may lose a lot of calcium producing egg shells, so they should have extra calcium supplementation, including a soluble supplement placed directly on the lips (see your veterinarian).

Males have large bulges at the base of the tail for the hemipenes and two enlarged tubercles behind the cloacal opening. Neither sex has femoral or pre-anal pores. A female lays two round hard-shelled eggs per clutch, and she is able to produce a clutch every two weeks until she runs out of stored sperm or depletes all the calcium from her body and drops dead. The eggs are laid on the ground in a moderately moist area. They should be incubated in a relatively dry incubator, not saturated vermiculite, and will hatch in about 56 to 60 days at 82°F. The young look like tiny Leopard Geckos and can climb until they gain weight. They need the smallest crickets and fruitflies to prosper as they are only 2 inches long. They grow rapidly

Madagascan Big-head Geckos, *Paroedura pictus*, are frequently captive-bred. Avoid wild-caught ones when possible. This is a hatchling. Photo by R. D. Bartlett.

and may be sexually mature in just six months, but should not be allowed to breed until at least ten months old. Keep the sexes separate from three months of age on unless you want very short-lived females.

Unlike most familiar geckos, the Madagascan Big-head is short-lived in captivity, seldom lasting more than three years. Assumedly this short lifetime is natural and not due to captive conditions. The species is captive-bred in fair numbers and is moderately popular. When albinos or lutinos with brighter colors appear, the species is likely to become more popular.

TURKISH GECKOS

The genus *Hemidactylus* is a gigantic and complicated one, with about 80 species described from Asia, Africa, and tropical America. All are small, under about 6 inches, and rather slender, with a long tail. There is much variation in the scalation of the species, from nearly smooth, with just tiny scales in regular

In the pet trade, many species of small geckos are called house geckos. It can be very difficult to tell which species is being sold. This is *Hemidactylus frenatus*. Photo by R. D. Bartlett.

row, to very rough, with many large pointed tubercles along the back and sides. The head is pointed, the eyes large and gold to dark brown, and the fingers and toes have wide climbing pads and large claws. Colors vary greatly, from uniformly pale tan to dark brown with bands of white spots across the back. Few of the species are distinguished by bright colors.

Many of these geckos have been spread around the world by trade, their eggs or even adults being carried from port to port in plants, cargo containers, and other

Hemidactylus flaviviridis is another of the house geckos. Generally speaking, the house geckos like warm humid enclosures. Many will only eat very small insects. Photo by A. Norman.

hidden spots. They have established themselves near seaports even in the southern United States, and may be abundant near structures with lights that draw many insects. They often occur in large colonies that are easy to miss during the day but hard to ignore at night. At least one species is parthenogenetic, producing viable eggs without mating.

Unfortunately, most of the Turkish geckos are sold as snake

This Turkish Gecko, *Hemidactylus turcicus*, has laid two large eggs. Because the young are so small, breeding the *Hemidactylus* species is very challenging. Photo by R. S. Simmons.

food at very low prices and often are highly stressed. In the United States specimens of several species are taken from introduced populations in southern Florida and shipped to pet shops. If not damaged (look for torn skin and missing digits), they may adapt well to terrarium conditions and provide a very inexpensive group of geckos for the beginner or specialist.

Currently we maintain a small colony of *Hemidactylus turcicus*, the true Turkish or Mediterranean

Although not highly regarded amongst hobbyists because of their small size and inexpensive cost, Turkish Geckos, *Hemidactylus turcicus*, are still interesting and attractive lizards. Photo by K. T. Nemuras.

Gecko, a 4-inch species whose original home was the dry shores of the eastern Mediterranean and the Red Sea. It is a pale whitish or sandy species with scattered dark brown spots over the back and legs. There are large pointed white tubercles on the sides and many rows of pointed tubercles on original tails. Few specimens have full tails, as they seem to drop them even during interactions with each other. Nocturnal, they are not disturbed by low light levels during the day and often can be seen clinging to the glass or the screened lid of their terrarium. Occasionally they become vocal, with a variety of squeaks and chattering.

The hard-shelled round eggs are laid on the ground or wedged into corners and bark. They hatch in about six to eight weeks into tiny (1.5 inches) young much like adults except the brown banding across the back is more definite. The young do not appear to be bothered by adults in the colony, and they soon are the same size as the adults. Sexual maturity is reached in less than a year. Males differ from females by having distinct pre-anal and femoral pores. Albinos are known.

This is just one of the many species of *Hemidactylus* occasionally available, and if you have the space you might want to give one a try.

WALL GECKOS

The African and Middle Eastern (with one species in tropical America) genus *Tarentola* contains over a dozen species of rather stout brown species with heavy heads covered with small scales. The fingers and toes have broad climbing pads; short claws are present on all but the third and fourth toes. Though several species occasionally appear in the hobby, one is fairly common and rather distinctive.

This robust and handsome lizard is a Moorish Gecko, *Tarentola mauritanica*. These hardy geckos are usually inexpensive. Photo by K. H. Switak.

The Moorish Gecko or Crocodile Gecko, *Tarentola mauritanica*, is a species of dry, rocky habitats along both coasts of the Mediterranean. Adults may be over 6 inches long and have a broad, flat head and eyes with golden irises. In adults the nape, back, and tail are covered with enlarged tubercles in regular rows, each tubercle with a keel or point; they may look much like tiny crocodilians, and they have a

This Moorish Gecko, *Tarentola mauritanica*, is shedding its skin. Many geckos will eat their skins afterward, but the reason for this is not known for sure. Photo by J. Merli.

bite to match. It is a vicious predator on any insects and invertebrates it can catch and is a fast runner and climber.

Sexes are difficult to distinguish, but males are very territorial and aggressive, which may be all you need to tell them apart. Never place two males in one terrarium. Females lay the usual two round hard-shelled eggs on the ground or wedged between rocks. They hatch in under three months if incubated at about 80 to 90°F on a dry substrate with low humidity in the incubator. Hatchlings are about 2 inches long and have distinct brown bands across the back, but these soon begin to fade into the indistinct sandy brown with brown spots pattern of adults. This gecko, unlike most, matures very slowly, and it may take five years to reach breeding condition.

Moorish Geckos are easy to care for if kept fairly dry, warm (80 to 90°F is best), and well-fed. They also are inexpensive for such a large and distinctive gecko, but captive-bred specimens seldom are available. If you don't mind the lack of color, this is a great species for the beginner. Remember that they can climb well, so securely cover the cage. They also bite well and should be handled with a bit of caution.

ROUGH GECKOS

Genus *Pachydactylus*, the rough geckos of southern Africa, is one of the most confused groups of geckos, but it contains many species with very pretty juveniles. However, because most come from South Africa and Namibia, which do not allow exports, they are not readily available. One species, Bibron's Gecko, *Pachydactylus bibroni*, ranges from the southern tip of Africa north into Angola and Tanzania and sometimes is included in shipments from Tanzania. This is a big (8 to 9 inches), very heavy-bodied gecko with a long, rather slender tail ringed with many rows of spiny tubercles. The back is covered with more than a dozen rows of

Bibron's Gecko, *Pachydactylus bibroni*, needs a hot and dry environment with plenty of rocks and branches. It is a hardy and long-lived species. Photo by I. Francais.

large round tubercles in regular rows, each tubercle with a strong keel; the tubercles are separated by the usual tiny gecko scales. There are strong ridges from the front of the eyes to the tip of the snout, and the scales at the back of the head may be enlarged and form an irregular spiny crest. Typical adults are pale brown with about five narrow brown lines across the back that are outlined with small white spots. Some specimens are uniformly dark brown, while others have distinct white-outlined dark brown blotches over the back.

Bibron's Gecko is an aggressive colonial species usually found in dry, rocky areas, living under rocks and on trees. Its toes have wide climbing pads, and it can move rapidly over vertical surfaces. They will take large and small insects, including crickets and grasshoppers, and are not averse to biting the hand that is feeding them. Large specimens will eat smaller ones, so they are best housed separately. If kept rather dry and warm, they make excellent and long-lived pets, though they seldom are bred in captivity. Females lay two hard-shelled slightly oval eggs wedged into cracks in bark or between rocks. This species, often confused with the Moorish Gecko, is available cheaply on occasion and, if in good condition, should be well worth the space and your attention.

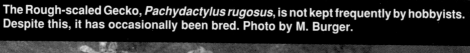

The Rough-scaled Gecko, *Pachydactylus rugosus*, is not kept frequently by hobbyists. Despite this, it has occasionally been bred. Photo by M. Burger.

ROUND PUPILS, GREEN BODIES

THE DAY GECKOS

Of all the geckos, probably few have developed as much of a mystique as have the day geckos of Madagascar and other Indian Ocean islands (with a single species in southern Africa). They are members of the genus *Phelsuma*, a complex group of lizards in which about 35 to 40 species have been described so far, some with subspecies, and one or two more are described every year or so. The vast majority of the species come from Madagascar, an island that rapidly is being cut-over and turned into small fields, while its fauna is shipped out to hobbyists before it all dies from lack of habitat. A quick check of a wholesale dealer's list received while writing this book showed ten species plus several subspecies for sale at prices ranging from $20 to $200 (retail would be double to triple the wholesale price), so there is no lack of variety for those with both small and large budgets.

The day geckos can be recognize by their small, pebble-like scales without enlarged tubercles on the back. The pupil is round, in keeping with their normal period of activity during the day and their frequent basking in sunlight. The tail is long and rather thick, with distinct hemipenis bulges at the base in males. Males also have a row of distinct pores extending from under one hind leg to the other without a break; in females pores if present are indistinct and irregular. Most of the species have bright colors, usually a greenish base with yellow specks and red spots, other red spots and sometimes stripes often being present on the head and at midback. The legs are short but strong, and the digits have wide climbing pads. These are quick-moving geckos that climb vertical glass surfaces with ease and can escape if you turn away for a second.

As a rule, the day geckos live in humid forests where they can have daily access to sunlight for basking, a humidity hovering near 60% to 75% during the day, somewhat more at night, and temperatures near 80°F. They tend to be arboreal, actively moving along tree trunks and vines, the males defending feeding and mating territories. In nature they feed on a variety of small invertebrates, especially insects, and also need nectar lapped from flowers. Water is lapped from leaves and also from small accumulations in holes in branches.

What this translates to in the terrarium is the need for a large (at least 20 gallons), preferably vertical terrarium with a substrate of soil and sphagnum or something similar to hold some moisture. There should be living plants with sturdy leaves able to support the weight of moving geckos, and there must be many climbing vines and branches. The terrarium must have good air circulation to avoid the growth of fungus. Mist the terrarium two or three times daily and maintain the temperature between 77 and 82°F during the day, with up to a ten degree drop at night. A small heating pad should be under part of the floor of the terrarium.

Unlike most geckos, day geckos like to bask and have a demand for both broad-spectrum fluorescent lighting and even a small basking light over a favored spot. Be sure that the geckos cannot gain access to the basking light. One of the most pathetic sights we've ever seen was a beautiful Giant Day Gecko that had managed to get to the basking light and burned a hole completely through one side of the tail base and through the femur of the hind leg. Lizards apparently cannot feel the pain of a burn (it must be alien to them, not being possible in nature) and will lie against a heat source until they literally burn to a crisp.

Feeding is much as for other geckos, with an emphasis on crickets, mealworms, and waxworms, but these geckos almost always need heavy vitamin and calcium supplementation. They also need daily offerings of honey water and fruit baby food, both with vitamins and more calcium added. Females (and sometimes males) store calcium in large sacs at the sides of the throat, being able to call on these reserves when they need to produce the thick, calcified egg shells.

Females lay the usual two round eggs that in almost all species are adhesive, sticking soundly in crevices in bark and between rocks. In a few species (none common in the terrarium) the female holds the newly laid eggs between her hind legs until they dry and then deposits them on the ground or may even bury them.

Day geckos should be housed separately both to prevent fights among males and also to prevent early matings that will lead to short lives for females. Like some other geckos, females can become egg-laying machines and die in just a year after maturing. Most species probably live several years in nature, with the large species surviving at least five years in the terrarium.

The common day geckos can be divided into two groups, the large species and the small species. Small day geckos usually are 2.5 to 6 inches long (males longer than females), while the giant species are 8 to 12 inches in total length (males also longer than females). The larger species generally are easier to handle than the small ones and certainly are less delicate and nervous. There are several authenticated reports of individuals of the small species dying when picked up, probably from the shock of being handled. They also have very delicate skins that are easily torn and lead to scars after healing. Like most geckos, the tail will be dropped if the gecko is handled too roughly.

GIANT DAY GECKOS

The most familiar, and also among the most affordable, day gecko is the Giant Madagascar Day Gecko, *Phelsuma madagascariensis*. This is a beautiful bright green to bluish or grayish green gecko commonly 8 inches long and sometimes 12 inches in total length. There usually are several blood-red spots on the back plus a red

Day geckos are beautiful but somewhat delicate captives. Research the needs of a potential purchase carefully before you bring it home. This is the Madagascar Giant Day Gecko, *Phelsuma madagascariensis grandis.* Photo by I. Francais.

stripe from the eye to the nostril and sometimes a bright red V on top of the snout. Several subspecies have been described, some of which probably are full species, others synonyms, and they vary from brightly marked with red as indicated to uniformly green with no pattern. The belly is whitish to yellowish.

Unlike most day geckos, this species often is able to adapt to deforestation and may be common in open forests at the edge of fields or even in villages. It is found in one color form or another over much of northern and eastern Madagascar.

Specimens like to bask and should be given about 14 hours of light most of the year, reduced to ten hours during the winter. They have a high metabolism and require constant heavy feedings for best health.

Females lay two eggs in a clutch and may produce six clutches per season at intervals of about a month. They hatch in a month at 82°F, producing grayish green hatchlings 2.5 inches long. The young may be snappy with each other and are best housed individually so you can be sure they are feeding well. They are mature in about a year.

STANDING'S DAY GECKO

Closely related to *P. madagascariensis*, Standing's Day Gecko, *Phelsuma standingi*, is found only in rather dry habitats of southwestern Madagascar. Like its relative, it reaches 12 inches in length, but it differs considerably

Standing's Day Gecko, *Phelsuma standingi*, is one of the largest day geckos. This one is demonstrating the head-down posture typical of day geckos. Photo by I. Francais

Unfortunately, the brilliant colors of this hatchling Standing's Day Gecko, *Phelsuma standingi*, will fade to the indistinct adult coloration in less than a year. Photo by R. D. Bartlett.

in color. Juveniles have a greenish head, bluish gray body, and bluish tail. There are narrow red bands across the back and the base of the tail, a unique and beautiful pattern. Unfortunately, as the gecko grows the colors fade and the red bands break into an indistinct network on a grayish background. This species can be kept much like the Giant Madagascar Day Gecko, though it likes it a bit drier and warmer, up to 90°F. Breeding in captivity is uncommon but not unheard-of. Only the juveniles sell well, as the adults are rather dull lizards.

THE GOLD-DUST DAY GECKO

One of the most attractive of the smaller day geckos is *Phelsuma laticauda*, a species of forests in northern Madagascar, with related species or subspecies on offshore islands and the Comoros. Adults are about 4.5 to 5 inches long, with a thick tail base that is somewhat flattened. The head and back are green, heavily spotted with tiny yellow spots only a scale wide. Some individuals are green with yellow highlights, but others are almost all bright golden

yellow. There are three red bands across the top of the head, three short stripes at the posterior part of the back, and some transverse red bands at the base of the tail. These colors sometimes are very subdued in older adults. There is a bright clear blue ring around the eye, sometimes reduced to a spot on the upper part of the eye.

Though small, Gold-dusts are just as aggressive as the other day geckos, so two males should never be placed in the same terrarium. A pair can be kept together in a moderately large, heavily planted terrarium. Their habitat must be humid (75% or more, but not wet) and warm (86 to 88°F) for best results. Spray daily with luke warm water. Provide them with the usual small insects plus sweet foods.

Attractive and relatively hardy, the Gold-dust Day Gecko, *Phelsuma laticauda*, is one of the most popular of the small day geckos. Photo by R. Zappalorti.

Although mixing species is always risky, in a large naturalistic terrarium Gold-dust Day Geckos, *Phelsuma laticauda*, usually will fare well with small anoles and small treefrogs. Photo by M. Burger.

Mating in captivity is not uncommon, and fair numbers are bred for the market. Females lay the usual two eggs that hatch in five to seven weeks at 82°F and humid surroundings. The hatchlings are greener than adults and need tiny insects as food. Females may lay a clutch every month, three or four months in a row, before taking a short rest. You might want to reduce the temperature a bit after the third clutch to make sure the female takes a break and thus leads a longer life.

Expensive and delicate, the Yellow-headed Day Gecko, *Phelsuma klemmeri*, should only be kept by hobbyists who have successfully kept other small day geckos. Photo by R. D. Bartlett.

THE YELLOW-HEADED DAY GECKO

One of the most unusual, uncommon, and expensive of the day geckos is the tiny *Phelsuma klemmeri* of northwestern Madagascar. Adult at only 3 inches in length, few specimens reach 4 inches. The coloration is striking and unique, being brown to turquoise blue over the back, continuing onto the tail, while the head may be bright yellow. There is a bright blue band on the upper side, with a nearly black band below. The throat is yellowish, the belly white; males may have a yellow spot over the vent.

This is an arboreal species that feeds on tiny insects and sweet foods and is just as aggressive as the larger species.

Unlike most other Madagascan day geckos, the two eggs are not adhesive, being laid in a hole in a branch or even near the ground. Hatching takes six to eight weeks depending on temperature, which can vary from 75 to 82°F. As you might expect, the hatchlings are extremely small (an inch long) and delicate, requiring only the tiniest of insects. There is some evidence that sex determination in this species is affected by incubation temperature, but details appear conflicting. Few hobbyists have the skill to maintain this species or the money to set up a breeding colony. Feeding often is difficult, and this is one of the species that has been known to die during handling.

Many other day geckos are available from time to time, but relatively few are bred in captivity, the hobby still being dependent

Handling Yellow-headed Day Geckos, *Phelsuma klemmeri*, is a very bad idea. They have been known to die just from gentle handling. Photo by R. D. Bartlett.

on imported specimens of most species. If the forests of Madagascar disappear before stable breeding colonies of most species are established, few species would remain in the terrarium. Species from other Indian Ocean islands generally are protected and are not available to the average hobbyist. Our advice is to start with a large species that is relatively inexpensive, trying to get a pair of captive-bred animals if at all possible. As you gain experience you can try your luck with smaller and more intricately colored species. Many hobbyists find the day geckos very satisfying to work with, while others have poor luck even with the larger species.

The Lined Day Gecko, *Phelsuma lineata*, is a frequently available species. This species should be kept humid with temperatures in the mid-80's during the day with roughly a 10 degree drop at night. Photo by P. Freed.

NOT AS RARE AS YOU THINK

With over 700 species, it is obvious that not all species of geckos are represented in the terrarium hobby. Probably over two-thirds of the species have never been kept in a terrarium, and fewer than a hundred are seen with any regularity. Many of the poorly known species are small brown lizards with few distinctive characters and really are appealing only to specialists. The following three groups, however, all are extremely distinctive in many respects of their structure and usually behavior, and all can be considered rare in the hobby. However, all are today being captive-bred in small numbers, though such adapted geckos may be very difficult to find and expensive to purchase. It is important to remember that just a few years ago both *Uroplatus* and *Rhacodactylus* were almost unknown in the terrarium, while today anyone with sufficient money and expertise can purchase a specimen or two and perhaps even breed them. *Teratoscincus* often still is imported in small numbers, but it seldom is bred.

The following three groups represent the extremes of development in the family Gekkonidae and perhaps also represent the future of the hobby.

WONDER GECKOS

Few geckos have large, overlapping fish-like scales on the body, and the Wonder Gecko, *Teratoscincus scincus*, is one of the few exceptions to the rule. This unique gecko belongs to a genus with only four species that vary from having normal fine scalation like other geckos to the extreme development in this species. The head is large, wide, with very large eyes; the head is covered with typical tiny scales. The trunk, however, is covered on the back and sides with only some two dozen rows of large overlapping scales that continue onto the tail. On top of the short tail is a row of very large plate-like scales down the center. There are eyelash-like scales to help keep sand out of the eyes, and the long fingers and toes have fine projecting scales at their edges to give increased traction in sand. Wonder Geckos also have been

Common Wonder Geckos, *Teratoscincus scincus*, are regarded as hard to keep. Make sure your terrarium setup is appropriate before you purchase this interesting animal. Photo by A. Norman.

called Frog-eyed Geckos, Fish-scaled Geckos, and Plate-tailed Geckos, all of which are appropriate; this is a gecko with so many strange characters that it is simply a wonder that it can exist.

The skin is exceedingly thin and tears even during careful handling, so this is not a species to be touched often. The body color varies from sandy yellow tan to pale bluish gray, with dark brown lines on the head and several jagged stripes on the body; the belly is white. Adults may be more than 6 inches long, but most specimens imported are somewhat smaller.

As you might expect from the presence of comb scales on the fingers and toes, this is a species of dry habitats, often sand dunes, where it burrows down as much as 12 inches to find a damp layer of sand. The range is broad, extending from the Arabian Peninsula to Iran and the Caspian Sea into western China.

Because of its unusual habitat preference, keeping a Wonder Gecko healthy in captivity may be difficult. One approach is to provide a 10-gallon terrarium with a layer of fine sand at least 4 inches deep, the bottom kept somewhat damp by adding water through small plastic pipes in the corners. Another approach is to simply provide a deep sand substrate and many hiding places on the surface, misting the tank daily to increase the humidity. These geckos like warm temperatures (between 80 and 90°F) and will require

supplemental heat through a heating pad under the terrarium. Let the temperature fall by ten or more degrees at night to duplicate cooling in the desert.

Feeding is much as in other geckos, emphasizing small insects of all types, especially beetles and crickets in this case. A vitamin and mineral supplement should be given once or twice a week. Pets may have a tendency to eat all the insects presented until they actually bulge, so control how many crickets they are given each week and do not allow them to feed until full—they will stop feeding only when ready to burst.

Breeding, which is rare in the terrarium, takes place early in the year following a cooling period of several weeks. Females lay a pair of round eggs with thin, delicate shells that really should not be handled. Incubation requires only a low humidity, under 50%, and takes two and a half to three months. The hatchlings are about 2.5 inches long and are yellowish

Small-scaled Wonder Geckos, *Teratoscincus microlepis*, rarely are available. Experienced gecko-keepers should attempt to breed them before they disappear from the hobby altogether. Photo by A. Norman.

with five or six dark brown bands over the back. A female may produce three or four clutches per season.

These incredible geckos are not commonly available, though sometimes they reach the market in fairly large numbers. They are not for beginners and may be frustrating even to specialists. The generally similar Fine-scaled Wonder Gecko, *Teratoscincus microlepis*, has over a hundred tiny scales across the back and is brown above with narrow dark brown bands over the back. Its giant eye gives it a remarkable appearance. Keep it much like the common Wonder Gecko and expect similar problems.

The Fantastic Leaf-tailed Gecko, *Uroplatus phantasticus*, is a small ground-dwelling flat-tailed gecko. They can be kept like the Henkel's Flat-tailed Gecko, *Uroplatus henkeli*. Photo by M. Burger.

FLAT-TAILED GECKOS

About 10 to 12 species of the genus *Uroplatus*, the flat-tailed or leaf-tailed geckos, are found in rain forests of Madagascar. None of the species is common, and some are known from only one or two specimens. Though they vary greatly in size (from 12 inches to only 3 inches), all have a similar general appearance. The head is very large, with a flattened snout and very large brownish to golden eyes; the pupils have four pinholes. The legs are long and thin, the digits usually strongly webbed. Their crowning glory is the tail, which is short (sometimes less than a third the length of the body), thin, wide, and somewhat prehensile. There is a strong constriction at the base of the tail, and the tail is easily lost. In nature the geckos spend the day clinging to trees in a head-down position; fringes on the lips and side of the body together with brown color patterns that may be striped or look like clumps of lichens and bird droppings give them complete camouflage. They are active only at night (a red light is recommended if you ever want to seen them in action), hunting for roaches, grasshoppers, crickets, and other insects, which are stalked and then deliberately chewed after capture.

Flat-tailed geckos are very delicate animals that react poorly to handling, movement near the terrarium, and variations in temperature and humidity. They are among the most difficult of all the geckos to keep for any period of time, and very few are bred in captivity.

One of the most commonly seen forms (if any species can be said to be common) is Henkel's Flat-tail, *Uroplatus henkeli*, a 10-inch species from northwestern Madagascar. It has been maintained with some success at about 72 to 82°F and up to 90% humidity. Females lay the usual

Henkel's Flat-tailed Gecko, *Uroplatus henkeli*, varies greatly in coloration. Some show large patches of white, like this one; others are more subdued, mottled in greens and browns. Photo by R. D. Bartlett.

pair of eggs that hatch in about three months and produce hatchlings 2.5 inches long. The eggs are placed under debris on the ground and are not adhesive. They must be incubated in a moist container at about 82°F. There have been relatively few hatching successes, and the young are very delicate and difficult to maintain. Perhaps as more captive-bred specimens become available they will adapt better to the terrarium and the average hobbyist can expect to

None of the giant geckos from New Caledonia are available to hobbyists frequently. This is *Rhacodactylus chahoua*. Photo by R. D. Bartlett.

have at least a chance of successfully keeping and breeding this or any related species.

THE GIANT GECKOS

The island of New Caledonia (north of New Zealand and southeast of New Guinea) has a unique reptile fauna consisting mostly of skinks and geckos. Among the most unusual of its geckos are the six species of *Rhacodactylus*, the giant geckos. (Recently several Australian species have been transferred to this genus, a step not accepted by all workers, most of whom

Leach's Giant Gecko, *Rhacodactylus leachianus*, needs a spacious vertical terrarium with plenty of climbing branches and high humidity in order to thrive. Photo by R. D. Bartlett.

consider *Rhacodactylus* to be endemic to New Caledonia.) They are very modified members of the subfamily Diplodactylinae, an Australian and New Zealand group, and they lay soft-shelled eggs about twice as long as wide (one species gives live birth). They are recognized by their large size (8 to 14 inches total length), with a large head, stout body, toes with wide climbing pads, and short, prehensile tails that may have an adhesive sucker under the tip. Coloration varies from brownish to greenish, often with complicated patterns of spots and stripes.

In nature these are exceedingly arboreal geckos that live near the tops of large trees in and near rain forests. They are active only at night, spending the day in treeholes and under the cover of leaves, so they are very difficult to collect. The traditional method of collection has been to spot a specimen or small colony at the top of a tree and cut down all the trees around the gecko tree, leaving the gecko tree for last. Obviously this destructive method of collecting cannot be encouraged, and all the species are considered threatened or endangered in New Caledonia, though somehow all still make their way to the terrarium hobby with regularity.

Seen on occasion are the Eared Giant Gecko, *R. auriculatus*, an 8-inch species with a rather long tail, odd projections at the back of the head, and an extremely variable color pattern; Leach's Giant Gecko, *R. leachianus*, a true giant at 14 inches and recognizable by the very short tail and usually variegated color pattern of ashy gray spots and stripes on a reddish brown background; and the Rough-snouted Giant Gecko, *R. trachyrhynchus*, a very stout 12-inch species that often is bright olive-green in color with rows of white spots over the body, plus enlarged, rough scales on the snout.

These are aggressive geckos best kept only as pairs, and even then the animals may attack each other and cause severe wounds, especially during mating. They need a large vertical terrarium that is heavily planted and also contains climbing branches. The humidity must be very high, so a moisture-retaining substrate such as orchid bark is recommended, along with daily misting. A wide variety of large insects are accepted as food, as are other lizards and pinkie mice. In addition, these geckos eat many types of fruits, and often young will display a distinct preference for bananas fed from the hand. Their large size and heavy teeth, plus aggressive temperament, mean that they can and will bite the hand that feeds them, often breaking the skin and even producing deep gouges with profuse bleeding.

Females lay two elongated eggs in a shallow hole in the ground. The soft shells allow the eggs to take in moisture during incubation and increase in size. Incubation periods range from about 50 days to 80 days, with most records being about two months. The hatchlings are 2.5 to over 4 inches long and take their first crickets two to four days after leaving the egg. Though most species mature in a year as in other geckos, *R. leachianus* and *R. trachyrhynchus* may need five years before reaching full size and sexual maturity. *Rhacodactylus trachyrhynchus* is one of the few geckos known to give live birth, producing two young 3 to 4.5 inches long. Males may attack and eat the young, which are guarded by the mother.